THE POWER OF POETRY

A Whisper Of Words

Edited By Daisy Job

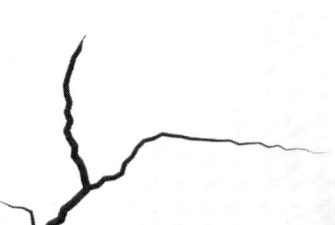

First published in Great Britain in 2023 by:

Young Writers
Remus House
Coltsfoot Drive
Peterborough
PE2 9BF
Telephone: 01733 890066
Website: www.youngwriters.co.uk

All Rights Reserved
Book Design by Ashley Janson
© Copyright Contributors 2022
Softback ISBN 978-1-80459-273-1

Printed and bound in the UK by BookPrintingUK
Website: www.bookprintinguk.com
YB0527L

FOREWORD

Since 1991, here at Young Writers we have celebrated the awesome power of creative writing, especially in young adults where it can serve as a vital method of expressing their emotions and views about the world around them. In every poem we see the effort and thought that each student published in this book has put into their work and by creating this anthology we hope to encourage them further with the ultimate goal of sparking a life-long love of writing.

Our latest competition for secondary school students, **The Power of Poetry,** challenged young writers to consider what was important to them and how to express that using the power of words. We wanted to give them a voice, the chance to express themselves freely and honestly, something which is so important for these young adults to feel confident and listened to. They could give an opinion, highlight an issue, consider a dilemma, impart advice or simply write about something they love. There were no restrictions on style or subject so you will find an anthology brimming with a variety of poetic styles and topics. We hope you find it as absorbing as we have.

We encourage young writers to express themselves and address subjects that matter to them, which sometimes means writing about sensitive or contentious topics. If you have been affected by any issues raised in this book, details on where to find help can be found at
www.youngwriters.co.uk/info/other/contact-lines

CONTENTS

Independent Entries

Yameena Jabbar — 1

Beckfoot Oakbank School, Keighley

Bronwyn Calvert (17) — 3

Broadwater School, Farncombe

Charley Stevens (14) — 4
Malna Horvath (12) — 6
Lee Armstrong (12) — 7
Aiman Ali (11) — 8
Cormac Fletcher (12) — 9
Rosie Day (12) — 10
Yamini Thaker-Wilson (12) — 11
Sonya Taylor (13) — 12
Holly Anscomb (12) — 13
Ellie Marin (12) — 14
Carmen Mato-Richards (12) — 15
Penelope Curtis (13) — 16
James Barnetson (12) — 17
Jacob Hammond (12) — 18
Nelly Stead (12) — 19
Cleo Harris (12) — 20
George Bannister (11) — 21
Ella Rowley (12) — 22
Annabel Bolton — 23
Marianna Drenos (12) — 24
Arthur Stanton — 25
Joseph Nottage (11) — 26

Cathkin High School, Cambuslang

Molly Payne (13) — 27
Heather Morris (13) — 28

Eastwood High School, Newton Mearns

Afaf Rabbani (12) — 29
Scarlett Williams (12) — 30
Fraser Gibb (12) — 32
Suhaana Mogal (11) — 33
Roma Jagdale (12) — 34
Elise Cruden (12) — 35
Lydia Watson (12) — 36
Adam Bishop (12) — 37
Nargiz Dauletkyzy (12) — 38
Ella Macdonald (12) — 39

Farringtons School, Chislehurst

Terasa White — 40

Frewen College, Northiam

Sophia Hepworth (14) — 42
Rufus Flynn (13) — 43
Sean Russell (12) — 44
Yanni Amos — 45
Isaac Colquhoun (12) — 46
Hayden Bradley (12) — 47
Isaac Prince (14) — 48
Jess Anderson (14) — 49
Lily Jacks (11) — 50
Paige Dodd (11) — 51
Sam Evans (13) — 52
Amelia Howard (11) — 53

Oscar Morton (11)	54
Talon Wright (11)	55
Oscar Bracken (13)	56
Nathanial Rhys Thomas (13)	57
Edie Flintham (11)	58
Raphael Bedwei-Majdoub (11)	59
Felix Henkel (15)	60

Fulham Cross Girls School, London

Marina Asaki (12)	61
Inaaya Aziz (12)	62
Taisa Rakowska (15)	64
Kiara Cummings (11)	66
Madeleine Maxwell-Gadd (14)	68
Aseel Said (13)	70
Javeria Saeed (15)	72
Aya Alkhatib (12)	74
Gracie Williams (11)	76
Amal Siddiqi (13)	78
Jasmin Zielinska (13)	79
Sarah Koudy (13)	80
Haya Abdullbasit (12)	81
Olimpia Milano (15)	82
Amelie Grandjean (13)	83

Our Lady Of Sion Senior School, Worthing

Selina Kinas-Kirk (15)	84
Iris Mallin (11)	87
Violet Mallin (11)	88
Louis Went (13)	90
Hope Bleker (11)	91
Max Taylor (12)	92
Amber Sisman	93
Harry Stoner (12)	94
Kyyen Nguyen	95
Zakir Khan	96
Mia Coughlan (12)	97
Ben Chapman (12)	98
Kyle Clapton (12)	99
Olive de Peyer (12)	100

Logan Tooth (13)	101

Our Lady Queen Of Peace Catholic Engineering College, Skelmersdale

Daniel Budgen (12)	102
Sam Flanagan (12)	103
Molly Peacock (13)	104
Alex Galiuk (13)	106
William Brown (12)	107
Lauren Roberts (12)	108
Oliver Geale (13)	109
Lucy Boden (12)	110
Taliah Fitzjohn (12)	111
Jack Dugdale (12)	112
Lexie Smith (13)	113
Maisie Fitzjohn (12)	114
Kaleb Johnson (12)	115
Poppy Farrell (12)	116
Oliver Gallagher (12)	117
Nathan Chane (12)	118
Fabian Adamczyk (13)	119
Bailey Hudson-Roberts (12)	120
Issy Hutchison (12)	121
Joshua Peters (14)	122
Paige Davies (12)	123
Ava-Lily McGrath (12)	124
Libby Barker-Gaskell (12)	125
Sophie Johnson (12)	126
Logan Grimes (12)	127
Olivia Niblock (12)	128
India Smith (12)	129
Anete Arbidana (12)	130
Holly Jameson (12)	131
Esmee Dutton (12)	132
Layton Lomax (12)	133
Ben Rimmer (12)	134
Rory Fenlow (12)	135
Connie-Mae Homson (12)	136
Grace Stannard (12)	137
Natalie Deegan (12)	138
Ryan Parry (13)	139
Jack Douglas (12)	140

Name	No.
Shayla-Mae Lewin (12)	141
Kyran Crosbie (12)	142
Charlie Poulton (12)	143
Leon Forkin (13)	144
Emily Boden (12)	145
Emily Johnson (12)	146
Tayla Caveney (12)	147
Kian Cooper (13)	148
Lucas Standrell (13)	149
Noah Connaughton (12)	150
Chloe Fitzpatrick (14)	151
Sophie McHale (13)	152
Courtney Felton (13)	153
Ryan Wright (13)	154
Mieszko Beczkiewicz (12)	155
Lexi Sultan (12)	156
Ruby Kervin (12)	157
Sadie Gleave (13)	158
Aimee Worrall (14)	159
Jessie Parker (13)	160
Amy-Dee Brow (13)	161
Thomas Massam (12)	162
Ava Tilley (13)	163
Liam Gadsby (13)	164
Roksana Spira (13)	165
Archie Elliott-Tynon	166
Libby Baines (13)	167
Lee O'Brien (13)	168
Darcey Kelly (13)	169
Brooke Fenney (13)	170
Lily Bennett (13)	171
Eva Nolan (12)	172
Aira Tetero (12)	173
Mikołaj Spyra (13)	174
Kerija Klauberga (13)	175
Ethan Dwyer (13)	176
Sarah Massam (13)	177
Dan Saver (13)	178
Leo Bacon (14)	179
Lily Heyes (13)	180
Oscar Finegan (12)	181
Connor White (13)	182
Lily Lowe (13)	183
Summer Chadwick (13)	184
Jack Bradbury (13)	185
Alfie Wilson (13)	186
Sienna Grice (12)	187
Ruby Lewis (13)	188
Leah Smith (13)	189
Aiden Fallon (13)	190
Lucy Gilbertson (12)	191

THE POEMS

The Things That Remind Us Of Home

I looked for words about moving on
Not from a person, but from a place
A place where I felt so at home
That the absence of my brother or mother bothered me
A place where we all sat down on the ground together
And broke bread at dusk and dawn
A place where we watched the sun come up from the hill
Whilst the heat burned my cheeks sore
Where I snuck down at 2 in the morning to let my brothers in
This strange small house on a hill in Yonkers
New York starting to feel to me like home
The crayon on the walls of the living room
Neon signs at the gas station, the small bathroom
The stained shower curtains, the cold couch
It felt to me a lot like home
I think I realise now that the poets only ever write
About moving on from people
But no one ever has the courage to talk about
Moving on from one's current state
A feeling, a thing, a taste, a smell
Small things that go unnoticed
The things that stay with us the longest

The things that remind us most of home
And I think it hits me now
That this is the last time we'll all be together
Again in the same city
Under the same roof the way we were today
The thing about time is that regardless of all circumstances
It heals all wounds
I've learned a lot from this trip
But I think one thing that will stick with me for life
Is that blood has always been thicker than water
And there's something about being amongst your own
That no matter where you go
Everywhere becomes home.

Yameena Jabbar

Green Leaves In A Grey City

Hanging from a window's edge,
Cared for as an endless pledge,
A green leaf in a grey city.

And now a few floors down
More pots with sprouts standing around,
Two green leaves in a grey city.

Homegrown herbs stretching for sun.
Fresh flavours in home cooking - it's begun,
Three green leaves in a grey city.

Slowly, they emerge across apartment blocks,
Converting high-rises into mossy rocks,
Hundreds of green leaves in a grey city.

Ancient oaks reclaiming land from lamp posts,
Metropolitan life becoming a ghost,
Thousands of green leaves in a grey city.

And when shop fronts look like terrariums
That's when we know Mother Nature is done,
When we have a forest in a green city.

Bronwyn Calvert (17)
Beckfoot Oakbank School, Keighley

Ke-Lee

Upon a typical night,
When the air felt cold
And the clouds moved like lost kites
You could feel the breeze growing old.

And walking down the forbidden street,
I saw a mysterious figure appear before me
I stared up and down to his feet.
He rotated his head 90 degrees.

Then he repeated with a robotic voice:
"My name is Ke-Lee... I have arisen -
You need to stop this domination
Look at yourself, pay attention and listen."

"Must you keep ruining, destroying this world?
Things are changing, you need to stop
This world belongs to me too
We are falling, falling like a raindrop."

"Stop wasting our home
Killing generations to come
It's a vicious cycle
It's like the world is a slum."

"My name is Ke-Lee
This is my message you must spread."

And just like that. Gone. Like a flea.
So, remember Ke-Lee's words. Remember them, please.

Charley Stevens (14)
Broadwater School, Farncombe

What Happened?

Is this really what the world has become?
The forests are being engulfed by flames
The ice caps are melting at a rapid rate
Smoke fills your lungs as you walk in cities
And plastic islands floating through the ocean

I thought that meadows would be filled with animals and deer
But Bambi's choking on a plastic bottle
Tears in its eyes as death comes near

I thought that there would be glaciers and ice caps in the sea
An environment for animals to be free
As the ice melts, taking the life of polar bears and more
Them holding on for dear life
As the ice melts below them, this never-ending strife

We are saying goodbye to so many animals
Farewell to koalas, tigers and narwhals
What happened to our once peaceful Earth...?

Malna Horvath (12)
Broadwater School, Farncombe

Global Warming

Greenhouse gases... just what the world needs
Absorbing heat and not letting go
The ice caps are melting
What will we do?
Let more greenhouse gases out is what we will do
We act like we care-
Let's face the truth, we don't
Forests are burning
Animals are losing habitats
What will we do?
We do it more
Nature is dying, I can prove it
When was the last time you saw a bee?
These big companies act like they care
They really don't
They open up more factories
Pump out more gases-
You think governments care...
They buy new houses on the beach
Take away other animals' homes
Oil pipes burst, killing birds-
We need to try and try and try.

Lee Armstrong (12)
Broadwater School, Farncombe

The World Needs Us

C limate change
L ook what you've done
I ce is melting in front of your eyes
M akes the weather more extreme
A nd there is no Plan B, is there?
T he climate is changing and the animals are dying
E veryone needs to act today to change the world or there won't be a tomorrow...

C hange your behaviour or it will be too late
H ave you seen what's going on?
A nd there is plastic all over the beach
N o turning back
G et a move on with your climate changes
E veryone needs to help.

Aiman Ali (11)
Broadwater School, Farncombe

Global Warming Poem

Global warming is destroying our planet
Petrol and diesel cars, we have to try to ban it
Deforestation has got trees losing bones
Monkeys and koalas have got disappearing homes
Sea creatures and turtles have got to avoid plastic
Polar bears are dying, we have to be more enthusiastic
Big cities pumping out CO_2
Surely there is something we can do?
Now there are growing deserts and wastelands
Come on, give the poor animals a helping hand
We don't have to give up hope
We can't let these animals choke.

Cormac Fletcher (12)
Broadwater School, Farncombe

The Final Hug

I was enjoying my day
The sun was peering down on me, scorching my furry back
Until... I realised
The sun was in my forest
Hugging my family tight
Overtaking all the trees as if alive
I heard the crackle and pop of the flames grow closer
I tried to run
When I looked up, I saw a family clutching onto each other
Like their lives depended on it
Their life did depend on it
I heard my baby brother cry
So I clawed at the tree
But as I felt the fire hug me tight
I got out a faint little... goodbye.

Rosie Day (12)
Broadwater School, Farncombe

Help

Help
I'm in a tree, frightened
Looking down upon a sea of fire
My home burning in front of my eyes
Fire and smoke are all I can see

I'm swimming in a sea of plastic
With a bag around my neck
I'm sinking and can hardly breathe
No one can help me now

I'm clinging to an ice cap
The last one I can see
So small I'm falling off slowly
And I can't swim back home

We are running out of time
But we are not out of hope
We can change the world
For the better, if we help.

Yamini Thaker-Wilson (12)
Broadwater School, Farncombe

Ukraine On Its Knees

A land full of wheat,
War is terribly indiscreet.
The clicking of guns,
Ammunition in tonnes.
An army to the north,
Comes and storms forth.

Kyiv besieged,
The world is on its knees.

That was months ago,
Blood followed.

Referendums soon,
Fitting a Russian tune.
A partial mobilization,
Ukrainian infiltration.
A diaspora population:
Exploded train stations.

Devoted to Ukraine,
Through blood. Through pain.
Zelenskyy stands strong.
Zelenskyy is not alone.
Standing for his home.

Sonya Taylor (13)
Broadwater School, Farncombe

Silent Night

Trees stand silent
They don't make a sound
Koalas sit up high
Trying not to be found
All is peaceful
All is calm
All is well
Habitats suddenly alarmed
The heat sweeps in and sets ablaze
Walls of fire build a maze
Thick fog lingers and trees set alight
The poor animals run in fright
Everything's gone
Everything's black
Now there is no turning back
The last surviving animals crawl in agony
We could have done better
We should have done better.

Holly Anscomb (12)
Broadwater School, Farncombe

What Do You Mean?

What do you mean the polar bears are fine?
Their home is melting
And their hearts are breaking
What do you mean the turtles are fine?
They're struggling in nets
Their shells are being mutilated
What do you mean the monkeys are fine?
Their trees are being cut
Their homes are being lost
What do you mean the fish are fine?
They are surrounded by plastic
Plastic is destroying their reefs
What do you mean the world is fine?
It's not.

Ellie Marin (12)
Broadwater School, Farncombe

No Second Chance

It's hard to breathe
The world's in sorrow
Some don't believe there will be a tomorrow

Yet it still isn't finished
The deal's not done
People can change
Everyone

Our future is almost stolen
And we are the thieves
We need to change our ways fast...
Our Earth is on fire we're in the past

The future is horrible
And we'll make it worse
But now we need to remove our own curse.

Carmen Mato-Richards (12)
Broadwater School, Farncombe

Rising Voices

The struggle to keep your head above the water
Becomes increasingly harder
When the water itself is rising.

The words cannot escape your lips
If the water surrounds you
So it's crucial to act. Before it's too late.

In the end, they'll realise you were foolish
Because you tried to stop the drowning
When you could have stopped it rising.

Penelope Curtis (13)
Broadwater School, Farncombe

Before I Die

Flames engulf me all around
As I watch the forest burn to the ground
My fur is singed
My vision gone
I hope I survive this
I hope it doesn't last long.

Flames creep closer to where I am perched
My time is up.
My head hurts.

I leave behind me
A koala family
Please let me see them
Just one last time
Before it's up

Before I die.

James Barnetson (12)
Broadwater School, Farncombe

The Fall Of The House Of Koala

Crackle! A burning sensation has awoken me
Mum? Dad? Daniel?

Crash! Fire everywhere ravaging the land I called home
The horrified screams take over my mind and make me blind

Daaaannnnn! Muuummm! Daaaddd!
Getting hotter and hotter
A ring of fire surrounds me

Monty? Dan? Monty goooo!
Noooo!

Crackle!
Crash!

Jacob Hammond (12)
Broadwater School, Farncombe

Fire, Fire

Fire climbing up my tree
No time for me to even flee
Submerged in black
Fire sets alight the forest behind my back
Family in trouble and dying around me
I'll be next, up there with them
Heat burning my paws
Clinging on to my home with only my claws
I think it's my time to say goodbye
No time for me to even cry
No time.

Nelly Stead (12)
Broadwater School, Farncombe

Nobody Knows

As the heat rises
And the cold decreases
And smoke becomes common
And rain is what we crave

Jumping on dirt
Instead of puddles
Walking along sand
And wishing for snow

As the world falls
And temperature grows
The world is suffocating
And nobody knows

The world will fall
And global warming will grow.

Cleo Harris (12)
Broadwater School, Farncombe

Deforestation And Pollution

When people cut down trees
(Don't do that please)
They turn it into fuel
But, listen to my call
It is not okay
Our planet will not stay
Fish are dying due to pollution
Let's stop this while it's in motion
Forests are being destroyed
Stop!
Or our planet won't be here to be enjoyed.

George Bannister (11)
Broadwater School, Farncombe

Ocean Damage

Plastic is bad for the environment
And putting sea creatures' lives in danger
There are less and less
Creatures in the ocean, and soon...
There will be none left
Recycle as much plastic as you can
And if you see any litter, pick it up
Don't be bitter, and pick up the litter!

Ella Rowley (12)
Broadwater School, Farncombe

The Saviour Of Me

I look at the ship
I begin to choke
I can not breathe
The plastic stops me

I start to drown
I can't get free
It went dark
The plastic stops me

A man dives in
I am freed
I swim away
More plastic stops me

I'm stuck again
The man can't reach me
The light is gone.

Annabel Bolton
Broadwater School, Farncombe

Our World

The world around us is slowly melting
The blue skies: now stale grey
The oceans were full
But are they now?

Oh, help our world.
Oh, our dear world.

Forests.
Skies.
Mountains.
Deserts.
Habitats:
If we destroy their homes - we go too.

Marianna Drenos (12)
Broadwater School, Farncombe

Just Cry

My home is being destroyed right before my eyes
Brothers and sisters falling down, plummeting from the sky
The fire is growing hotter, why God, why?
My friends and family all are lost, will I stay alive?
So, I cry
Just cry.

Arthur Stanton
Broadwater School, Farncombe

Don't Kill The Planet

Why do we harm the planet?
It's done nothing to us.
There's nothing called planet plus.
We destroy this home... for what?
I don't see the point.
Maybe there is no point.

Joseph Nottage (11)
Broadwater School, Farncombe

Una Maud Victoria Marson

U na Maud Victoria Marson, born in Jamaica 1905
N ever let the colour of her skin stop her
A lways determined, she knew what she wanted to do

M agazines she wrote
A nd spoke on the radio too
R eally passionate about feminism and writing poetry
S he married in 1960 but sadly passed in 65
O ther than her career, she left an impact on the world by...
N ever giving up.

Molly Payne (13)
Cathkin High School, Cambuslang

Ivory Bangle Lady

The lady rests amongst goods and gold
A blue glass jug, once so bright and bold
With bangles and pendants
With earrings that glow
From a warm place
She comes, she goes
North African history
A light, she glows.

Heather Morris (13)
Cathkin High School, Cambuslang

Deforestation

Deforestation - forests all clear
Small helpless animals lying in fear
Oceans, seas and dirty rivers
If you saw you would get shivers

Litter and rubbish everywhere
Selfish people don't seem to care
Lifeless animals left to die
It gets worse and worse as time passes by

Whole animal species are at risk
It is a problem we must fix
Climate change is causing floods
On our hands is all this blood

Come on now, let's all stand up
Come on now, let's raise our cups
It is our choice to try our best
We must face this with our chest

This problem is a huge case
It's our duty to make the world a better place
We have to try all we can
So everyone can live happily: child, woman and man.

Afaf Rabbani (12)
Eastwood High School, Newton Mearns

Fly Free

Oh, to fly free!
To swoop!
To dive!
Free of these
Pressing
City
Walls
As tall
And far
As the eyes can see

I want to break free
To be free
To fly free
Away from these dirty, litter-filled streets
Away from the scream of cars
Big black
Monstrous
Fumes coating my lungs
Closing in
Choking me
Chest heaving
Snatching air

The iron grip of the city
Killing me

Slowly
Squeezing
Constricting

Let me go!

I need open air
Space
To fly
Spread my wings
Be myself
Breathe

Breathe the fresh air!
Sing!
Let the notes flow from my being
Like golden sunshine turned liquid

Fly free!
Swoop and sing!
Dive and throw notes to the wind!

Be free!
Fly higher than the clouds
The sun
The stars!

Scarlett Williams (12)
Eastwood High School, Newton Mearns

Nature

A slight warm breeze hits the grass
I never want this summer to pass
A single leaf falls from a tree
As you hear the waves crash against the rocks at the sea

I hear the raindrops patter against the ground
As it makes a very beautiful sound
A very wet rock lies pointlessly on the floor
As I see the tide comes in on the seashore

A deer majestically skipped across the road
As the fireflies flying glowed
A buzzy bee landed on a flower
Then sadly mum said we had to go in an hour

I felt the sunshine on my face
As I thought to myself what a wonderful place
And now my poem comes to an end
But experiencing nature I would highly recommend.

Fraser Gibb (12)
Eastwood High School, Newton Mearns

Believing In Yourself

Every day doubting yourself
Whether or not you should
Or shouldn't, do or don't?
So many questions about
Yourself. Wealth, health, work and study
Always looking down
Comparing yourself to others
Being smothered in hate
Three words you should hear
Not only you have this fear
"Believe in yourself!"
Never lose hope. Nope, nope, nope
Always believe that you can achieve
You are enough
You are trying your best
Keep that fire burning in your chest!
Looking beyond all the rest
Being unique is what you seek
Keep all these things in mind
And happiness, you soon will find.

Suhaana Mogal (11)
Eastwood High School, Newton Mearns

Calling Out Sexism

I'm calling out sexism
I just want to say
That stereotypes and expectations
Are never okay!

You can't judge someone based on their looks
You cannot read people like they are books
Your visual expectations
May be pleasing to the eye...
But clearly, you have forgotten
How people are on the inside!

Boys can be this, while girls are to be that
Our futures are not to be dictated
We are all free

Don't chain people to the ground
Keep in mind
We are only human
Inside and out

So, I'm calling out sexism
I want to make a change
I want the world to be equal
Let's get on the same page.

Roma Jagdale (12)
Eastwood High School, Newton Mearns

Save The Turtles

Dive into the never-ending sea
Turtles in the deep blue ocean
Swimming in the plants and reefs
Gliding smoothly with every motion

They swim through long wavy seaweed
Unaware of the dangers ahead
Blindly sweeping through the leaves
Go any further and they'll end up dead

A young turtle leads the way
Dipping and diving, having a play
When all of a sudden, it comes to an end
Wrapped in plastic, unable to bend

Suffocating
Slowly dying
It's too late now
Left there lying

Stop what you're doing!
Stop these horrible notions
Recycle your litter
Save our oceans!

Elise Cruden (12)
Eastwood High School, Newton Mearns

Clouds

Giant clouds, floating about
So high up in the sky
Flying up there from dusk 'till dawn
I love watching you drift by

On hot and sunny days
In lakes and oceans, you lie
But when it's cold you move upwards
And when you come back down
It's no longer dry

When I look up high
I see you up above
Swaying through the sky
Like a beautiful dove

I wish I could join you up there
Oh so far away
But I can't, as I can't fly like you
So down on the ground, I'll stay.

Lydia Watson (12)
Eastwood High School, Newton Mearns

The Tall Mountain

Oh, tall mountain
How do you stand
And stay so tall
And never fall?

You stay so tall
After being battered
By wind and rain
You withstand the pain!

And being stood on
Walked all over
By foot after foot
Boot after boot.

How do you do it?
Oh, mighty mountain
So tall and proud
Reaching the height of the clouds!

So tall mountain
How long have you existed?
It could have been for a millennium
Or just since yesterday!

Adam Bishop (12)
Eastwood High School, Newton Mearns

Hope Is Not Last

I look out the window
And scare myself
All trees were cut
And animals were dead
The light is burning my pale hands
The planet is now black and dark
But in my heart, there is a spark

Now I begin my story
By telling people
The water was shining
And all the trees thriving

But that is the past
And our hope is not last
We can make a difference
By fixing from the very start
Feel this message in your heart.

Nargiz Dauletkyzy (12)
Eastwood High School, Newton Mearns

Global Warming

200 years ago...
Good morning!
Lovely day!
Oh, what a wonderful place to stay!
Bees a buzzing!
Ants working!
Ladybugs walking along!

Now...
Why is everything so warm?
Always cloudy
Run from disasters
More fuel needed
I wish polar bears weren't going extinct
No natural beauty in sight
Going extinct and we're too late to do anything.

Ella Macdonald (12)
Eastwood High School, Newton Mearns

The Woods

The brown leaves
Like moth wings
Fluttering down to the moss
Landing softly like a butterfly on a feather
The light shining through the trees
The stepping stones pathed the way through the pitch-black
Leading through the leaves
Crunching like snow under my feet
As I walked through the decaying woods

The bitter cold
Jack Frost biting against me
My fluffy gloves
Drenched by the snow
Snowmen and their family waving at me
As I walked through the frozen woods

The new cherry blossoms
Filling the air with the fragrant smell
The yellow daffodils
Blue skies
The fresh water rippling
As I walk through the aromatic woods

The hot sun
Melting my sun cream off
The woodpecker stabbing at the oak

Red foxes scuttling through the green grass
The green leaves
On the tall trees
As I walk through the green woods.

Terasa White
Farringtons School, Chislehurst

You Call That Wildlife?

What is wildlife? you ask,
Well, wildlife was animals or plants living, growing
In their natural environment.
Untouched by human disruption.
It was Mother Nature's gift of perfection.
Wildlife was all around us filled with humble bumblebees
And thriving skydiving dragonflies.

It was butterflies that flutter on rosy cheeks
And vines that would have grapes the colour of limes.
But you see, my dear, that was when harmony and
Humanity were one. Now there is no harmony or love
For the animals and those humble bumblebees
No longer buzz.

Sky-high dragonflies weep and suffer because
Of our mistakes. So you ask, what is wildlife?
Well, my dear, I can't tell you what is wildlife
But I can tell you what it was.

Sophia Hepworth (14)
Frewen College, Northiam

Big, Big Promise

Earth, Earth, we stole its worth,
It's just like a witch's curse.
And now I write this lonely letter,
To call on you to make things better.
Maybe, just maybe if we try,
Our baby will not cry,
Because we're helping the Earth die.
Long ago, we told a lie,
That we could all live together,
Perfectly balanced like a feather.
So please just try before the Earth dies,
So stop and help us save the world,
As if we were Santa's little elves.

Rufus Flynn (13)
Frewen College, Northiam

Kindness

Kindness to all animals,
No matter if they are a mammal, bird, fish, crustacean, reptile or amphibian,
We are all living beings,
Treat them with respect, not as garbage,
Treat them how you would want to be treated,
Kindness to all animals,
No matter if they are a cow, dog, snake, shark or spider,
We are living beings
And we need to change how we treat animals
And each other as well,
And we need to stop hunting endangered species.

Sean Russell (12)
Frewen College, Northiam

Earth

Look out of your window, you will see a nice day,
You might think to yourself, *hmmm, everything fine.*

But there is a sad, dark truth...
The ice is melting as we speak,
Places are flooding,
Plastic is drifting in the sea.

So...
Next time you look out of the window,
Think to yourself about what's happening on our planet,
So try to not throw away your empty water bottles,
And recycle them!

Yanni Amos
Frewen College, Northiam

Natural Beauty

You could roam the green hills in old England,
Or you could walk through the snow in Finland,
You could climb the mountains in Scotland and see a kelt,
But in a minute, you might melt.

You could explore the coastline of Wales,
And gaze at the different sea snails,
You could go to Greece,
And feel the peace.

Every country you explore in the world,
You'll always find beauty and animals.

Isaac Colquhoun (12)
Frewen College, Northiam

Stop Abusing Pugs

Stop abusing us just for the money,
It hurts us too much,
We just want a warm, cosy bed,
And a decent owner to feed us,
Because half of us haven't had this decent feeling,
Please just stop annoying us and someone listen to us,
Some of us haven't even been out of our cages for months,
Some of us haven't even managed to play with a bone,
As we've just been left here and mistreated.

Hayden Bradley (12)
Frewen College, Northiam

Stop Passing The Blame

We're all globally going nobly,
Everything at our fingertips,
Taking what made Earth worth it,
And shoving it out of the way for faster devices.
We are doomed,
Don't deal with the devil.
We as a species have killed our planet,
And there is no going back.
It's all going black.
We did this,
Stop passing the blame,
Lose the fame,
And get a shovel to move the rubble.

Isaac Prince (14)
Frewen College, Northiam

The Sea

The sea,
Surrounded by wave breakers and holidaymakers
Home to swift snappers and dancing attackers
But the big blue basement is being ruined
By these holidaymakers
The hard skeleton of the coral is breaking
And the sea turtles are choking
And the cocktail of colour is fading
The aquamarine sea is being destroyed by submarines
And the golden beaches are being ruined by our bleaches.

Jess Anderson (14)
Frewen College, Northiam

The Black Hole

Swirling in the wind, curling in the sky,
As a hurricane comes by.
A twisting horror,
That makes the Earth shake and crumble,
A disastrous fog,
You can see nothing,
So brown and dark,
A tall, scary monster,
A twisting, turning tunnel as scary as a black hole,
Just one trip and you could fall.

Lily Jacks (11)
Frewen College, Northiam

Animal Abusing

C ruel owners abusing animals
R escuing sad animals
U nkind hands
E very animal wishes for a loving home
L onging for food and warmth
T ime is going by as more animals lose their homes
Y oung homeless animals.

Paige Dodd (11)
Frewen College, Northiam

Do Your Part

The Earth needs your help, it's old and tired,
You can help, just be inspired.

So much pollution,
There's always a solution.

Help the nation,
Get to your station.

Do your part and the Earth,
Will realise its worth.

Sam Evans (13)
Frewen College, Northiam

Otter

O ver the water where otters reside
T hey swim and play and duck and dive
T heir webbed feet, thick dense fur
E ating fish and causing a stir
R acing and chasing - oh, what a life.

Amelia Howard (11)
Frewen College, Northiam

MrBeast

Team trees, team seas,
Beast burgers and Feastables
Removing trash out of the sea
Donating money to charity
Giving to people on the street
He has lots of money but
He uses it wisely.

Oscar Morton (11)
Frewen College, Northiam

The World

The town needs help
So do we and the sea
Don't forget about me
So we can be free
Okay don't forget me
I help you breathe
So why not help us
So we can help you.

Talon Wright (11)
Frewen College, Northiam

The Swamp

The swamp so very dark
Giving me a question mark
Through the mangrove bark
The fish pray in the moonlight bay
Disobeying nature's way
Wondrous things happen in the swamp.

Oscar Bracken (13)
Frewen College, Northiam

Overpopulation

Overpopulation
Is clogging up the nation
There is too much migration
For vacation
Which makes fumigation
Of carbonation
There is infestation
Of the human nation.

Nathanial Rhys Thomas (13)
Frewen College, Northiam

Spring

Trees singing, vines dancing, leaves fluttering,
Red roses reflecting moonlight like a pearl.
Birds flying while tweeting, growing trees,
Flowing seas, beautiful flowers.

Edie Flintham (11)
Frewen College, Northiam

Space

Space is a great big place,
It contains species like the human race.
At the centre of the universe,
There is a small planet called Earth.

Raphael Bedwei-Majdoub (11)
Frewen College, Northiam

Mole

A kennings poem

Mountain maker,
Hole creator,
Worm eater,
Light hider,
Soil mender,
Lawn killer,
Earth mover.

Felix Henkel (15)
Frewen College, Northiam

Earth Calling For Help

We can't waste a minute
We pollute the air
We cut down trees
When Earth is calling for help
The ice is melting
Unpredictable weather
This happens because of us

We can't waste a minute
Factories giving out toxic chemicals
Rubbish dumped on the road
When Earth is calling for help
Wildfires caused easily
New World Record of highest temperatures
This happens because of us

We can't waste a minute
But we still have hope
If we act now
At least something will change

Earth is calling for help
And there is only one thing to do

Help is on the way.

Marina Asaki (12)
Fulham Cross Girls School, London

Climate Change

Climate change was created by mankind

A thick blanket of fire
Wrapped around the Earth like a burning hug

Our world has changed
Once a young puppy with nothing but love
Now a bloodthirsty canine, ready to pounce

Our planet has turned into an irreversible nightmare brought to life
Breaking the world's newest record of highest temperature
Because of us
Haunting our regrettable decisions like a ghost

Deforestation is one of the reasons
Why our planet has dramatically warmed up

Billions of animals have been killed before losing their homes
Because of us

Does it make sense to burn down the forests
Cut down trees which we breathe from
Kill animals along with destroying their homes?

Let's not forget the fact that the world is heating up
So much that glaciers are melting

Causing floods to such an extent that people are dying
If we keep this up, there will be nothing left
Of the Earth but the water

It is our responsibility to protect our planet
And everything that lives on it

Let's stop this depressing, life-shattering hell that we are creating
Absentmindedly to ourselves
And human up and face the biggest problem in the world
To pay favour to the generation to come

Save the planet!
Save the animals!
Save mankind!
Spread the word!

Inaaya Aziz (12)
Fulham Cross Girls School, London

Mass Extinction Event

Imagine a day where
We look outside to grey
Imagine a day when
The green's gone away
Hope gone when the last
Bee lays its wings
This is what humanity brings

The adept amur leopard
Hunts in the cold
The black-footed ferret
In its grassland home
Someone must've said
Do not kill the Hawksbill turtle
With African forest elephants
Still in dense forest homes
But how long will they survive
Too close to where humans roam?

The Tasmanian tiger died captive and alone
This marsupial could not roam; could not go home
Chile sandalwood captivated
With its attractive scent
It attracted so much
That it brought upon its torment

The laughing owl lost its chase
When a new competitor entered the race

The Permian-Triassic killed
Over 90 percent
This event...
Earned its 'Great Dying' name
It brought so much pain
CO_2 rose from eruptions below
From the Siberian traps
Which wrapped the Earth
Hidden from the sun
252 million years ago
Earth could not grow
And will this be our turn to go?

Our end beckons
In the time of the world, we have seconds
So many are gone or nearly left
Species descend
Humans content
So I guess we're the next
Mass extinction event.

Taisa Rakowska (15)
Fulham Cross Girls School, London

A Human

I'm not here as a student
Nor a female, nor child, nor an Asian
I am what I was born... a human

Police brutality, stabbings, shootings
All because of the colour of one's skin
Because of their gender
Because of their age
And where they grew up
Why is it that we get judged by a difference that makes us unique?
Makes us who we are?

Why are we still loomed into a society
Where we are looked down upon?
Imagine being called racial slurs at the age of 11
Before you've gone one month into your new secondary school
Before you've even started your life

Does your life really mean anything
If Malala didn't give you that right to an education
Or if the suffragettes didn't give you that right to vote
Did George Floyd willingly give up his life over police brutality? No.

Racism is learned, gender inequality is learned
Hatred and discrimination are learned
We need to come together to stop it

I am what I started off as... a human.

Kiara Cummings (11)
Fulham Cross Girls School, London

Eventually It Stops

Dull the noise, press your hands against your ears
Overwhelmed by the racket, are you?
The snapping of shackles
Of cuffs, of labels, on those you seek to oppress
Utter nothing about the reek
Why not punish us, prohibit them, push him closer
Closer to his own, early grave
And keep her to the side, or in the corner, or outside the room
Whatever suits you best
As long as you don't hear the screams, the pleas, the riot
The storm, the sigh. The reek
It stings your eyes, but no tears will be shed
That makes you like them, the ones you oppress
That's right, push harder against your ears
Stop the noise, squeeze your eyelids shut
Stop the stench, drown it out
Don't let yourself feel what they feel
Don't let yourself feel
The reek tickles your nose
Irritated, you sniff
It only brings it seeping in further
Move your hands
Open your eyes
To see, not hear

No, you don't hear
Because the world went quiet a long time ago

Tell me, does it sting?

Madeleine Maxwell-Gadd (14)
Fulham Cross Girls School, London

I Wish

Beauty is as much a blessing as it is a curse
They told me people would die for your face
They told me people would die for your body
They told me how lucky I am
They told me I should be happy
So I smiled and acted as they told me
But this mask has become my shackles
And now I'm under this curse of Beauty
Will all of this change if I become ugly?
But I was born this way
And everyone has their own beauty
So am I under a curse
Or are we all?
When will the curtains fall
On this miserable play?
Free me from this curse...
But who will free me
Other than me?

Is beauty a blessing or a curse?

But I think it's a blessing
Yet I still ask myself if beauty is a blessing or a curse
Since everyone has it - it must be a blessing
They just haven't realised because they can't

See how bright they shine
In this dark world…

Beauty is a blessing, not a curse
But how can I be sure?

Aseel Said (13)
Fulham Cross Girls School, London

Freedom

They say it's a bird which flies high
But I am not a bird who can soar
Nor am I a fish of the sea
I am but a human
So what does it mean to be free?

Freedom
They say it's a sight only some may see
So what of the bird with no wings
Or the fish with no sea
And I - a human - trapped by society?

Caged within these four walls
And even if I were to escape
I'd be chained by this earth's laws
So what if I were to go beyond and explore infinity
Would I ever truly be free?

Such as a kingdom without a king
How can there be freedom without hope?
For it's this indoctrinated heart it seems
Which confines me to the laws of humanity

Too much freedom and I am lost
Too little and I am trapped

So where can this bird learn to soar?
Where can this fish roam its sea?

Where can this human finally be free?

Javeria Saeed (15)
Fulham Cross Girls School, London

Social Media

TikTok, Instagram
It's all a waste of time
Facebook, Twitter
A deleterious crime

You may not notice it yet
But slowly you will find
How addictive this issue is
And how it affects your mind

These detrimental useless apps
Were made to keep you scrolling
You could've done so much more
Like painting, exercising or sewing

Getting a notification
Or posting a video
Releases dopamine
The happy hormone

Your brain will compare you
To those on social media
Your self-esteem will decrease
Even though it's all filters

Melatonin is the hormone
That helps you fall asleep
Blue light, which is from your screen
Causes melatonin to decrease

These points are not all
The downsides of social media
If you want to know more
Then I recommend doing some research.

Aya Alkhatib (12)
Fulham Cross Girls School, London

Girl

    I am **G** reat
    I am **I** ntelligent
    I am **R** espectful
    I am **L** oyal

I am me

    I am **G** orgeous
    I am **I** mpeccable
    I am **R** adiant
    I am **L** oving

I am me

    I am **G** ood-hearted
    I am **I** ndependent
    I am **R** elentless
    I am **L** ikeable

I am me

    I am **G** enial
    I am **I** mportant
    I am **R** esourceful
    I am **L** ively

I am me

I am **G** ifted
I am **I** nsightful
I am **R** ight-minded
I am **L** egendary

Throughout everything, I am ME.

Gracie Williams (11)
Fulham Cross Girls School, London

The Future

Hidden in the mists of time
Awaiting for the right time to shine
Dream your future from which you cannot wake
As it is just a blink away...

You may not be able to see the future but
Whether it's high or low, it's really up to you
There are no limitations, just the unknowns

The future never speaks
But when it reaches the peaks
You will know that it's here
As it will be crystal clear

And when it comes
You will succumb
To what the future brings
When it takes wing.

Amal Siddiqi (13)
Fulham Cross Girls School, London

Our Earth

Our trees are burnt and chopped down
Our oceans are polluted and losing lives
Our air is not the same as it used to be
All because we want more than we need

When more cars are used
And more rubbish is burned
Carbon dioxide is released into the air
And killing our Earth

Animal testing
Animal hunting
And animals suffocating on plastic bags
All because we want more than we need

Take this time to stop and think
How can you save our Earth?

Jasmin Zielinska (13)
Fulham Cross Girls School, London

The Xinjiang Internment Camp Victims

Our silent screams have deafened my ears
With our blood-filled tears
Every body that drops
It feels like the world stops

After every dusk and dawn
I wonder if our attention will ever be drawn
As we pray for hope
I wonder if we will ever cope
With this repeating nightmare?

Sarah Koudy (13)
Fulham Cross Girls School, London

Save The Earth

Save the Earth
Save the seas
Save the animals
Save the trees
Say no to a planet B
Save the parks
Save the plants
Make your mark
Keep your precious planet clean
The pressure's on you
What will you do to save your future?
Save the animals
Save the seas
Save the animals
Save the trees.

Haya Abdullbasit (12)
Fulham Cross Girls School, London

I Wish

I wish I wrote the way I thought
Obsessively
Incessantly
With maddening desire
I'd write until my breaking point
I'd write until the break of dawn
Novels spiralling out into the abysmal nothing
And I'd write about you more than I should.

Olimpia Milano (15)
Fulham Cross Girls School, London

Climate Change

I thought it was plain
Black and white, what a concept
It's complicated

It's complex but important
This is our safety net
It's my world

Let's make my world
Beautiful again
Let's have hope.

Amelie Grandjean (13)
Fulham Cross Girls School, London

Man Overboard

Everything comes to an end
That won't change
However the length of time we decide to
Prevent this 'end' is completely up to us

We are walking, humankind
Walking along this plank
So fragile, so fine
But we walk
The danger doesn't cross our minds

This earth we live upon
So beautiful and free
The air wafting through all the numerous trees
Yet somehow, we still selfishly
Take advantage of this wondrous discovery

So we walk some more, along this plank
Ignoring all the signs begging us to turn back
The creaks and sways felt beneath our feet
They mean nothing to us
Nothing to our greed

Uncontrolled and unwanted civilisation
The outburst and eruption of population
The congestion that us humans we cause
A new word in our dictionaries, pollution

In the air and in the seas, just pause,
And think about what this could have been

So now we're halfway along this plank
The unsettling noises, the water rushing along the riverbank
But oblivious, we decided not to turn back
We take a step over the developing crack

The protests begin
And realisation kicks in
The small worries in our lives
Become erased and instead lies
The biggest worry of them all
Our Earth, and her fall
We don't deserve to call her ours
Not after we brought about her scars

Still, humankind ignored and forgot
The trend in all charts the scientists plot
All the warnings and cautions we got from the start
We didn't listen to
We never took it to heart

Now we are past the turning points
We spent too long collecting coins
Our screams and begs invade the noise
Now we would give anything just to stop the clock
To jam our words and actions between the hands
So time can stop, just let it stop…

But we took that fatal step
Pushed everything we've ever known to the edge
And finally, that crack made a snap that all will forever recall

Man overboard...

The biggest threat is us
Do something soon
We can never just assume
That we too, won't fall.

Selina Kinas-Kirk (15)
Our Lady Of Sion Senior School, Worthing

If I Ruled The World

If I ruled the world
The sun would shine brightly
Sky would be forever blue
Birds would sing their upbeat tunes
While small kids played with eco-friendly balloons

If I ruled the world
We'd have respect for all - Black, trans, female or bi
The world would be boring with just you and I
Kindness and love would fill all the darkness
Hurt and hatred would never be heard of

If I ruled the world
Chocolate would be sold in every shop
We'd have unicorns and fairies bringing joy without stop
Santa would bring extra presents each year
And we'd all ride dragons to school - no fear

If I ruled the world
And made this fantasy come true
I'd need you, you and yes, you too
If we all work together as a unified team
Then this strange and destroyed world we can redeem

If only I ruled the world
It wouldn't just be a dream.

Iris Mallin (11)
Our Lady Of Sion Senior School, Worthing

Our World

Our home is dying and I don't know what to do
The oceans are rising, the fires are blazing, the wind is howling
The extinction list is way too high
And I don't want to say goodbye
I don't want to end up like the dinosaurs did
I don't want to give up hope
We can't snap the rope
That holds all the Earth together
We can't snap the rope
That carries all of our lives
We can't snap the rope
That keeps us all alive
There is no Planet B
Earth is our home...
But what if the extinction list gets even higher
And humans are added?
And I won't know what to do

2044, the Earth is no more
The Arctic ice has melted
And there is no going back
The climate is hotter than hot
The worries of our home are in one big tangled knot
As the world leaders look back in regret
At their countries, now a mess

We don't know how to turn back
We don't know what to do

Unless
Our home still can be saved, we'll find out what to do
The oceans will stop rising
There will be no more fire
And we'll stop the temperature getting higher
The extinction list will be at an all-time low
And trees will be everywhere
And we'll stop polluting the air
We won't need any Planet B
As Earth is our home
And Earth will always be our home
You know what to do...

Violet Mallin (11)
Our Lady Of Sion Senior School, Worthing

World War

The world is dying due to pandemics and poverty
Illness and irony, lockdown and climate change
It's gone really bad, war and crime, fake news and lies

I hope it gets better, it's not looking good though
They're destroying the world with politics, pollen
and pollution
Starvation and dehydration, killing animals and people alike

The world's like a soldier or person like us through war
But we're like a virus killing it from inside

The sky was blue, now red
People were happy, now sad
Animals prospered, now they're slaughtered

We're like a virus, eating away at the world
Like a disease, we're killing it with no return
So it's bound to end, just not like this

Ice caps melting and coral reefs dying
Fish dying and birds failing at flying.

Louis Went (13)
Our Lady Of Sion Senior School, Worthing

2044

A world we knew
A world we once knew
A world we have ruined and scuffed with our shoe
A world we bruised black and blue
A world we've reduced to watery goo

A planet that is a planet no more
A planet that ended in 2044
A planet that isn't as it was before
A planet we've neglected and decided to ignore

We haven't treated it with care
We've pumped harmful gases into the air
There is no planet B, as we are aware
Yet we are pushing to the point of no repair

However

If we search hard enough to find
An answer to our ever-growing crime
We could spend what is left of our time
Doing what we know is kind.

Hope Bleker (11)
Our Lady Of Sion Senior School, Worthing

The Environment

E very animal deserves a chance
N o animal should deserve to be killed
V anish the violence and make peace
I f we are all being owned, would we like it?
R arely do I see a wild horse or pig
O ld or young, you can still make a difference
N ot just animals but mankind too
M an and creature should be at one
E ach one of us has a voice to share
N ature should be left untouched
T rees and leaves count as well, so be the bigger person and help save our planet.

Max Taylor (12)
Our Lady Of Sion Senior School, Worthing

Climate Change

There's nothing we can do
Don't you dare say that
There is hope

Trust me, it's true

It's gone too far
Don't believe that
We can change our old ways

Trust me, it's true

The temperatures are rising
The animals are dying
The sea levels are increasing
Our environment is ceasing

We can never change
It's wrong to say
We still have chance

Trust me, it's true.

Now read this poem backwards.

Amber Sisman
Our Lady Of Sion Senior School, Worthing

The War On Earth

They're destroying our plants
This isn't a game of chance
We need to change
Before everything looks strange

Remember the climate is changing
We need to start engaging
So here's your call
Before it's irreversible

We need to work as a team
To make a new scheme
The sun is getting hot
So we need to boycott

The trees are getting the chop
While we bury it at the shop
So don't get distracted
Before everything is extracted.

Harry Stoner (12)
Our Lady Of Sion Senior School, Worthing

Signs From The Sun

Ever since you left
The weather has been dull
Just overbearing clouds
And unremarkable greys
But today, it was different
An alluring display
Ambers; pearly pinks
Spiralling together, a cacophony of hues
A sign of change
That I'm finally letting go...
A sign of hope
That my worries will fade...
A sign of the times
That ends *our* past and starts *my* new beginning
As this sunset does the same
And welcomes the night sky.

Kyyen Nguyen
Our Lady Of Sion Senior School, Worthing

Never Give Up

Never give up
It's not always just luck
Remember to give it a try
Even if you are feeling low or high

If you get it wrong the first time
Always put yourself back in line
If you feel like you're never gonna get it right
Try again and put up a fight

Resilience is key
Even if it's tricky
Always try again
It's never quite the end

Winners never quit
Quitters never win
The rule is to never give in.

Zakir Khan
Our Lady Of Sion Senior School, Worthing

Save Our Planet

Our world is dying
Animals are crying
We are lying
But I am trying

I see nature's beauty
From far away it looks pretty
Saving the planet is our duty
But only I am trying

We litter our rubbish
When we shouldn't
We have damaged our world
And we shouldn't be doing this

Please save our planet
Because there is no going back
The time is ticking
We don't have a plan B.

Mia Coughlan (12)
Our Lady Of Sion Senior School, Worthing

Our World

Trees were green, big and strong but now they're not
We got it all wrong
The sky was blue, now is grey
Will it forever stay?
Ice caps are melting, polar bears are crying
Please save them from dying
Chickens were free and now in a cage
I bet they feel enraged
The rivers are droughted
We're starting to be doubted
Storms are rising
Houses are flying
Please save the planet
Before it's too late.

Ben Chapman (12)
Our Lady Of Sion Senior School, Worthing

Environment

There's no time
To solve this crime
We need to change
Before it's out of range

We need to act
Before we're trapped
The world is warmer
Everyone's in trauma

There's no time
There's more and more crimes
The trees will fall
We need to recall

We need to act
There's no turning back
There won't be more quacks
Instead, we're left with cracks.

Kyle Clapton (12)
Our Lady Of Sion Senior School, Worthing

Save Our Planet

The world is dying
Our brains are frying
We need to change our habits
Save our planet!

The world is breaking into shards
It's no longer rock hard
We need to plan it
To save our planet!

We aren't thinking straight
So can it
Before it's too late
Save our planet!

The world is dying
Our brains are frying
We need to change our habits
Save our planet!

Olive de Peyer (12)
Our Lady Of Sion Senior School, Worthing

A Habit We Need To Change

The gas is overwhelming
I know it's a habit
Even though you can't grab it
The planet is drying up
And the animals are frying up
The trees can not take the heat
In about a year, they'll be beat
And we can not repeat.

Logan Tooth (13)
Our Lady Of Sion Senior School, Worthing

JMO

The JMO has bright green football pitches in Skelmersdale,
People play many fun and exciting sports at the JMO,
It is next to loads of roads that connect to it.

The football pitches are gigantic and exciting,
The goalposts are tall, wide and white,
It has lots of long grey roads that connect to a car park.

I can see beautiful green grass that I can't believe is fake,
It is as durable as metal and has little black bits in-between the astroturf that sneak into your football boots.
I can see the massive white goalposts.

I can hear the loud cars passing by like rockets in space,
I can also hear people having a great time, chatting and laughing.
I feel calm and excited when at the JMO.

And I,
Feel like I'm at home and I belong at the JMO,
And I think this is the best place on Earth,
And I imagine people and teams playing football and training.
The JMO has football pitches in Skelmersdale.

Daniel Budgen (12)
Our Lady Queen Of Peace Catholic Engineering College, Skelmersdale

Global Warming

As the ice caps melt and the polar bears begin to die,
People speed past in their cars and don't even try,
Don't even try, try to help, help with the cause of the planet,
We have been warned, but don't seem to care, almost as if we planned it,
Our coastline cities begin to submerge and sink,
So does the ice in the ice rink,
We are running out of time, time to think,
Think about the consequences of when we sink,
The forests are burnt, burnt to the floor,
Which makes species extinct, more and more,
Our deserts get wet, wet and wetter,
And there is nothing to do to make it better,
All of our biomes seem to change,
It's not hard to spot, we can see it from range,
All the animals are receiving harm,
And the oceans and seas are getting less calm,
The sharks and fish have more space to swim,
This, for us, is not a win,
Global warming is a serious thing and should be taken seriously.

Sam Flanagan (12)
Our Lady Queen Of Peace Catholic Engineering College, Skelmersdale

Our Actions Have Consequences

The loss, the sorrow, the pain, these are caused by our actions.
We need to take control, we need to fix the pain we caused.
Animals' lives being tragically taken, their homes going up in flames
As their land gets destroyed.

The pain we need to feel knowing in fifty years' time, little children,
Possibly your own kids,
Will never get the experience of seeing tigers, lions, zebras, nothing.

Only empty land. Only the lifeless feeling of a once jovial place
But now a dead atmosphere.
Only pain knowing we caused innocent animals to go extinct.
Knowing we caused these animals to go extinct.
Knowing future generations might never see certain wildlife.

We need to take action now before it's too late.
We need to save our wildlife and our Mother Nature.
We need to save our world.

We need to take back control.
We need to fix the problems that we caused.
Help us save our world.

Molly Peacock (13)
Our Lady Queen Of Peace Catholic Engineering College, Skelmersdale

My Story

I've been gone for a couple of months, I had to get my head straight,
Depression got the best of me, I'm slipping away.
I'll be lying on my bed looking up to the Lord
Like I don't wanna die young, but you can take me today.
Cut my wrists a few times just to help the pain,
But self-harm ain't a phase, it cuts deep in my veins.
And my friends don't understand, so they look at me strange,
But who am I to blame when I'm feeling this way?
I'm just an angel, tryna get home and find my place,
I'll wonder what it takes just to open Heaven's gates,
Or am I going to Hell, confessing my mistakes?
Got tears on my face, man, I pray for better days.
And my bro was 15, 8 years in the grave,
I should message his bro like, I hope you're okay,
And your little brother's safe, put some food on his plate.
They don't check up on me or say, "How was your day?"

Alex Galiuk (13)
Our Lady Queen Of Peace Catholic Engineering College, Skelmersdale

The Museum

The museum has artefacts to see and it is in Liverpool,
The ancient artefacts go back centuries ago or sometimes millions of years ago,
But this very museum is in Liverpool.

The museum is strong, hard, solid, brave,
And its most important use is to stop the rain from wetting the inside,
But it is also used to store artefacts, paintings, stuffed animals and bones.

But some colours you might see that'll want to shimmer in your eyes are white, grey, red and yellow.
You might hear the people scream if the birds caw as it hits midnight and the darkness falls upon us,
But you will still hear the soft sound of the wind whistling behind you, but this is supposed to make people hope and feel happiness.

And I might not like museums much,
But this one place stores the memories of animals and people who lived thousands of years ago,
And you know it exists in Liverpool.

William Brown (12)
Our Lady Queen Of Peace Catholic Engineering College, Skelmersdale

City Life

Cars pass by as people walk on broken paths,
In this big city, bright lights, wrecked kites in this big city,
Screams of fun, things that must be done, you must come!
Shops full, doors pulled, are you ready to have fun?
Roller coasters run, friends lead a ton,
I'm going to ask again, are you having fun in this big city?
Concerts are loud, people are proud from this big city.
People fall in love, as they should,
Everyone is having fun in this city.
Billboards help up high, advertising in the sky,
But why in this big city?
But this has an effect on this big city.
Fog's in the sky, breathing becomes a try.
In this big city, prices are high, oh my.
Everything has an impact on this big city.

Make your move today,
Every little bit of help,
Still makes a change.

Do it before it's too late,
In this big city.

Lauren Roberts (12)
Our Lady Queen Of Peace Catholic Engineering College, Skelmersdale

Halloween Fright

It was Halloween night,
A killer had escaped,
No one knew his name,
So we called him the Hollow Knight.
He was all over the news,
Everyone was inside with nothing to do.
He just kept killing and killing,
Everyone had had enough.
Me and my dad went around looking for him,
We were going to end it tonight.
We had heard he was in Sorrow Street,
We were going to lure him back to our house,
And attempt to finish him once and for all.
This was the only way that this would end.
We had him,
All we had to do was lock him up,
And destroy our house with him inside.
It was finished.
We had to put gasoline everywhere,
And set it on fire.
This was the end.
No more Hollow Knight!
Everyone was chanting in joy,
Everyone was finally safe.
That's what everyone thought...

Oliver Geale (13)
Our Lady Queen Of Peace Catholic Engineering College, Skelmersdale

The Beacon At Its Finest

The Beacon has tall, majestic trees engulfing it,
People stroll through the scenery on big walks,
It sits intimidatingly beside different housing estates.

The Beacon is serene and transfixing,
The Gruffalo stands in the woods, tall and realistic,
The park is fun and huge and filled with children.

Green, brown, red, black, blue and silver,
I can hear the sounds of the trees swaying,
And mischievously whispering to each other in the breeze,
When I am there, I feel calm, happy and adventurous.

And I,
I imagine that some of the old ruins are a witch's house,
And there are robbers lining the old cobbled streets behind the trees, ready to jump out and steal from you.
The Beacon has tall, majestic trees engulfing it.

Lucy Boden (12)
Our Lady Queen Of Peace Catholic Engineering College, Skelmersdale

Change For All

Changing our world, what a hard thing to do,
Especially when no one has told you...
The temperature rises every day
And all we are doing is watching our world fade away.
Money and fame overtake the social world,
Why do we think this isn't absurd?
Homes flooded, crops ruined, summer's way too hot,
I can't believe the corporations can't see how bad the climate has got.
The oceans spill like a fallen cup,
Man, we really are out of luck.

We have let the future down,
Leaving them to be bound with a permanent frown.
Capable of change yet we never do,
All 'they' care for isn't what's best for you.
Now we've made the generation cry,
Leaving our precious world to die...

Taliah Fitzjohn (12)
Our Lady Queen Of Peace Catholic Engineering College, Skelmersdale

The Beacon Point

The Beacon Point is an old abandoned building,
People walk up it for a lovely walk and sensational views,
The Beacon Point is located on the outskirts of Skem.

The Beacon Point is an old, abandoned, mysterious building with beautiful, emerald green trees,
At the bottom is an old abandoned church building with a look that sends chills down your spine,
It's mostly green in all different shades,
With pine, oak and birch all dancing away in the air.

You can hear the wind racing away through the sky,
The atmosphere is sensational,
You feel relaxed, happy and just tranquil.

And I,
I imagine the Vikings fighting out here,
The Beacon Point is an old abandoned building.

Jack Dugdale (12)
Our Lady Queen Of Peace Catholic Engineering College, Skelmersdale

Animal Abuse

Cruelty to animals is getting worse,
But nobody seems to care,
The RSPCA are trying their best,
But it's still not fair.
Animals don't understand,
Abuse should be banned.
Animals just want lovely warm cuddles,
Or to even have fun in muddy puddles.
Whoever dares to do this should be put in jail,
But never be bailed.
Animals need someone to know that their safe,
The world is just not a nice place.
Don't have a pet if you don't even care,
They need a lot of your time and most of your day,
And sometimes they even love to lay.
You have to take them on daily walks,
And promise to care for them forever,
Animal abuse needs to stop!

Lexie Smith (13)
Our Lady Queen Of Peace Catholic Engineering College, Skelmersdale

The Breakfast Cafe

There's a place called Liverpool with a breakfast cafe,
This cafe has outstanding food with children running,
Under the cafe, there is a carpet shop, very cramped,
Small and feels safe, it's cosy enough to feel like home.

The posh decor makes me mesmerised,
Expensive food but worth every penny,
Cosy colours like brown and beige.

The sound of people talking and the plates crashing,
As soon as I step inside,
I feel hungry from the smell of the food,
Jackets off, it's really warm.

And I,
I imagine my happy place and soon have no stress,
It's like no other,
There's a place called Liverpool with a breakfast cafe.

Maisie Fitzjohn (12)
Our Lady Queen Of Peace Catholic Engineering College, Skelmersdale

Filled

In Manchester city centre, there are shops filled with people scavenging for things to buy,
Crowded streets filled with children screaming,
And parents shushing in the centre of Manchester.

The giant, standing centre filled with brands and greasy food,
As the people scurry for food, the restaurants begin to fill with miles,
You can see the floor, the deep brown bricks filling the cracks in the floor.

As the streets fill up, you can hear the sound of hustle and bustle filling your ears,
You can feel the excitement but the anxiety at the same time.

And I,
Feel my arms getting tighter and tighter,
As I begin to break down in Manchester city centre.

Kaleb Johnson (12)
Our Lady Queen Of Peace Catholic Engineering College, Skelmersdale

Save Our World

C limate change is impacting our world
L oving animals will lose their lives
I ce caps are melting
M alaysia have a big impact on deforestation
A mazon rainforest is steaming because of the heat
T igers are becoming listed creatures
E cosystem can be saved

C aring animals are losing their homes
H elp our planet and the animals in it
A mazon rainforest is discovering climate change
N ext generation won't see animals we did
G reenhouse gases aren't a joke
E xtinction is a big thing nowadays.

We cannot let this carry on.
Act fast!

Poppy Farrell (12)
Our Lady Queen Of Peace Catholic Engineering College, Skelmersdale

The Liver Building, Liverpool

The Liver Building stands and guards Liverpool,
You can go around on the electric scooters to the shops,
They are right next to Merseyside where all the boats stay.

The liver bird graciously guards Liverpool,
The lights around the building glisten brightly at night,
The Liver Building is stood there firmly in the ground.

You can see grey and black but at night, this city is colourful,
You can hear the car engines and seagulls hollering,
I feel happy, there are fun things to do, especially at Christmas.

And I,
Imagine the liver birds are watching you all the time,
The Liver Building stands and guards Liverpool.

Oliver Gallagher (12)
Our Lady Queen Of Peace Catholic Engineering College, Skelmersdale

The Concourse

In Skelmersdale, the Concourse is popular,
Every day, people are shopping shop to shop,
At the Concourse which is in the centre of Skelmersdale.

The structure of the building is tall and long,
The car park is big and wide,
The shops at the bottom are small and wide,
But the ones at the top are big and long.

When you look at the Concourse, you see all different colours around,
The noises coming from inside are the shoppers hustling and talking,
But when I see the Concourse, I feel comfortable.

And I,
I feel like I'm at home when I see this place,
And in Skelmersdale, the Concourse is popular.

Nathan Chane (12)
Our Lady Queen Of Peace Catholic Engineering College, Skelmersdale

Joe's Life Story

R ough neighbourhood, that's where he grew up
E ating food was a gift, no one tried giving a lift
S aid he loves life - deep down, the boy wants to die
I n his cell, the only time he's seen his father
L iving with his auntie 'cause his mum passed away
I n a cell aged 12, that's all he thought about
E ven now when he says I made it, his mother is who it's aimed at
N ew people coming, I don't trust anyone - life's a game, but I beat every one
C ompetition around me but I know I'm the best
E verybody sees the outcome, no one sees the come up.

Fabian Adamczyk (13)
Our Lady Queen Of Peace Catholic Engineering College, Skelmersdale

Tawd Bike Park

In Skelmersdale, the Tawd reveals a bike track,
You ride your bike from jump to jump, not being aware,
It is next to the high school, Our Lady Queen of Peace.

The track's surroundings are quiet and hidden,
The steep jumps scattered along the trails,
The blue flowing river around the area.

The green leaves on the tall trees remove any sun from nature's floor,
You can hear the relaxing noise of the rushing stream,
I feel relieved from any stress within me.

And I,
I can imagine myself showcasing my tricks in front of millions of people,
In Skelmersdale, the Tawd reveals a bike track.

Bailey Hudson-Roberts (12)
Our Lady Queen Of Peace Catholic Engineering College, Skelmersdale

The Dock In Liverpool

The dock in Liverpool is bursting with people,
At the dock, people go from shop to shop looking for things they need to buy,
Near the dark River Mersey.

The dock is loud and packed,
The shops are big and full,
And the fountains are quiet and peaceful.

I see an overload of colours as the painted rocks tower over the dock,
I hear shoppers rushing around as the River Mersey flows in the background,
I feel happy as I walk around this place deciding what to do.

And I,
I imagine workers long ago building all the museums and shops for us to use,
The dock in Liverpool is bursting with people.

Issy Hutchison (12)
Our Lady Queen Of Peace Catholic Engineering College, Skelmersdale

Corruption Of Our Crust

E vil is changing our world for good
N ow is the time to act
V ery powerful people are corrupting the world
I t's time to administer some justice
R eal effects do exist
O n the Earth's crust
N ow is the time, now is the time for change for us
M en and women come together
E verywhere you can
N ow it's time to do some good, it's
T ime for us to act
A ll of us, even you, come together now
L ine us together, for the greater good, for the world, for now, corruption of the crust, we need to fix it now!

Joshua Peters (14)
Our Lady Queen Of Peace Catholic Engineering College, Skelmersdale

The Concourse

In Skelmersdale, lies the Concourse,
In the Concourse, there are lots of shops,
People go from shop to shop looking for things to buy,
The Concourse is in the centre of Skelmersdale.

The building is tall and beautiful,
The Concourse has Home Bargains,
The Concourse is near the swimming baths.

I can see the grey, shiny floor as I look down,
I can hear people chatting and the sound of the till,
I feel excited to see what's in the shops.

And I,
I feel like I'm at home,
In Skelmersdale, lies the Concourse,
In the Concourse, there are lots of shops.

Paige Davies (12)
Our Lady Queen Of Peace Catholic Engineering College, Skelmersdale

Climate Change

It's our responsibility to look after our home,
So why are we treating it as something that's not our own?
The world is beginning to change,
Which is so very strange.
But who is to blame for our planet being set to flames?
No, you and I can't make this stop,
But small changes will put us on top.
The ice caps are melting, polar bears are sinking,
Sea levels rising, sending cities drowning.
As the atmosphere thickens, the heat can't escape,
Leaving nowhere safe.
We need to make a bend in the path we are walking
Before this becomes the beginning of the end...

Ava-Lily McGrath (12)
Our Lady Queen Of Peace Catholic Engineering College, Skelmersdale

Liverpool One

Liverpool One is a shopping centre,
People use this facility to shop, eat and gather like schools of fish,
It sits in the centre of Liverpool.

Liverpool One is crowded and busy,
The shops are full and overwhelming,
Families are stressing checking train times.

The colours you can see are subtle, grey, white and black,
You can hear the conversations of groups and the buskers singing.

And I,
When I'm there, I feel joy but I'm overwhelmed,
All I can imagine is young children playing in the Victorian era,
Liverpool One is a shopping centre.

Libby Barker-Gaskell (12)
Our Lady Queen Of Peace Catholic Engineering College, Skelmersdale

A World

A world that's great,
A world of peace,
A world that is perfect,
A world that we need.

However, this world is damaged,
By fossil fuels that are used,
That change our weather,
That could never be better.

To the twirling winds,
Or the water that covers the land,
Maybe even the heatwaves,
Those ice caps that get melted in the north and south now.

This is corrupting our planet,
And needs to be stopped,
Before 2050,
And our world is lost.
So hear me now when I beg please,
We need to protest against those thieves.

Sophie Johnson (12)
Our Lady Queen Of Peace Catholic Engineering College, Skelmersdale

Skelmersdale Cinema

The cinema in the Concourse has movies that anyone can enjoy, young or old,
The cinema lives in the heart of Skem.

The cinema has randomly patterned carpets and an ancient projector,
And four small TVs showing all the movies playing inside…

The colours I can see are black, white and red.
The sounds I can hear are people munching on sweets,
I feel delighted to see the Minions.

And I,
I feel like I am enjoying the movies,
I imagine I am one with the Minions,
The cinema in the Concourse has movies that anyone can enjoy, young or old.

Logan Grimes (12)
Our Lady Queen Of Peace Catholic Engineering College, Skelmersdale

Can We Fix What We Have Done?

C limate change is impacting our world
L ife will never be the same
I ce is melting, taking animals' habitats
M any animals' homes are getting destroyed
A nimals are dying
T igers are beginning to go extinct
E xtinction

C hange for the better, and help our world
H elp our planet, and fix climate change
A nimals are suffering
N o escape until we try and make a difference
G ive our world a chance
E very animal should deserve a home.

Olivia Niblock (12)
Our Lady Queen Of Peace Catholic Engineering College, Skelmersdale

Reduce, Reuse, Recycle

Reduce, reuse, recycle,
All the things we need to know.
Reduce, reuse, recycle,
Now everyone give it a go.

Reduce, reuse, recycle,
Cardboard, paper, glass or plastic.
Reduce, reuse, recycle,
If we all did this, it'd be fantastic.

Reduce, reuse, recycle,
It would make Earth a better place.
Reduce, reuse, recycle,
The happiness would show on your face.

Reduce, reuse, recycle,
So before you throw anything away.
Reduce, reuse, recycle,
Ask yourself, can it be used differently someday?

India Smith (12)
Our Lady Queen Of Peace Catholic Engineering College, Skelmersdale

The Trafford Centre

The Trafford Centre has many shops,
In the Trafford Centre, people go to explore the shops,
This is in the city centre.

The Trafford Centre is loud and busy,
The Trafford Centre is surrounded by other buildings,
The Trafford Centre booms with people.

In this building, I can spot the warm colour of beige,
I can hear the hustle of people scurrying around,
I can feel the sense of excitement rushing through my veins when at this place.

And I,
I feel free and let loose,
The Trafford Centre has many shops.

Anete Arbidane (12)
Our Lady Queen Of Peace Catholic Engineering College, Skelmersdale

The Old Oak Tree

The old oak tree stands in peace,
Most of humanity, ignoring its pleas,
Asking for help, it moans and groans,
Watching its friend tumble down just down the road.

Inevitable to dying, the animals cry,
Wanting to help, the oak tree tries,
Instead, the old oak tree gets itself in trouble,
As the carbon dioxide it consumes begins to double.

The old oak tree frolics in the breeze,
No one realises the help nature needs,
The old oak tree starts to fall as its life is too tough,
For no person is brave enough.

Holly Jameson (12)
Our Lady Queen Of Peace Catholic Engineering College, Skelmersdale

The Liver Building

The building standing tall and beautiful above me,
The clock ticking and waves washing in the sea,
Gracefully in the River Mersey.

Protective and outstanding, the building stands,
Where the liver birds sit up high,
The seagulls fly and land.

Waves splashing, footsteps stepping,
And people muttering as they shop,
And the sound of loud ticking clocks.

And I,
Safe, I feel safe and at home,
As I look and gaze at this building made of stone,
The building standing tall and beautiful above me.

Esmee Dutton (12)
Our Lady Queen Of Peace Catholic Engineering College, Skelmersdale

The Liver Birds On The Liver Building

The liver birds on the Liver Building,
Staying still in the cold breeze of the wind,
Near the River Mersey.

The building is gigantic and pretty,
The shops glow with their items,
Trees around this beautiful place swoosh and rattle in the wind.

Colours of it shine like never before,
You can hear the muttering and mumbling of the people inside,
It feels like I have pride in this stunning place.

And I,
Imagine that the birds protect everyone in Liverpool,
The liver birds on the Liver Building.

Layton Lomax (12)
Our Lady Queen Of Peace Catholic Engineering College, Skelmersdale

Save Our Planet

N ow countries heed the warnings
O ur planet is officially warming

P oints of ours all to be heard
L et our cries be known
A t the state of our Earth
N ear enough to the end
E nd the factories, end the warming
T o save our home

B eware, there is no Planet B, beware, beware, beware

Coal keeps on burning
Our goals are not working
But countries still do not listen
There's no going back now
Our own planet is getting ruined.

Ben Rimmer (12)
Our Lady Queen Of Peace Catholic Engineering College, Skelmersdale

Beware, Beware, Beware

All countries heed my warning
The entire planet is warming
All leaders be concerned
Otherwise, you may get burnt

All countries heed my warning
The entire planet is warming
All animals far and wide
Are trying their best to hide

All countries heed my warning
The entire planet is warming
Stop burning so much coal
Unless you want to dig yourself a big hole

All countries heed my warning
The entire planet is warming
Listen to this poem now
Otherwise, you may drown.

Rory Fenlow (12)
Our Lady Queen Of Peace Catholic Engineering College, Skelmersdale

Deforestation

D ark early mornings building homes
E arly mornings collecting supplies
F orests getting demolished
O ld cosy homes are gone
R emaking homes to sleep
E ach creature needs a home
S ome go hunting, others build
T ime being wasted finding new homes
A nimals losing their homes
T rees releasing oxygen are now gone
I n them are hundreds of animals
O n the trees, there are thousands of creatures
N ature is the best.

Connie-Mae Homson (12)
Our Lady Queen Of Peace Catholic Engineering College, Skelmersdale

Climate Change

Our planet is dying,
The sea levels are rapidly rising.
But no one seems to care,
And continue to pump carbon into the air.

We are destroying our atmosphere,
But no one can hear...
Our planet needs our help,
Our ice caps will continue to melt.

Many breeds of animals going extinct,
But we don't care to think,
Animals losing their home,
A place they used to roam.

Our planet needs help when heating at rapid rates,
We need your help before it's too late!

Grace Stannard (12)
Our Lady Queen Of Peace Catholic Engineering College, Skelmersdale

Liverpool

Liverpool has many shops,
People go to the shops to find things they want to buy,
Liverpool is just outside of Skelmersdale.

The town centre is packed, full and exciting,
The museums are ancient, interesting and valuable,
The cafes are well-known and used.

There are a variety of colours spread across Liverpool like a rainbow,
You can hear the subtle voices of the people,
I feel happy when I am there.

And I,
I feel free when I am in Liverpool,
Liverpool has many shops.

Natalie Deegan (12)
Our Lady Queen Of Peace Catholic Engineering College, Skelmersdale

Powered Winds

A big, tall tower standing high,
Painted in a clear, shiny white.
Its blades spin quite fast,
And its structure shall forever last.
The paint will always shine,
As well as powering the time.
Though it is easily heard,
And is a danger to flying birds,
They stand tall in groups,
Powering ovens to heat up soup.
What is this behemoth, you may ask?
A wind turbine, helping power the automation of tasks.
Part of this poem may not rhyme,
But its message is as straightforward as a line.

Ryan Parry (13)
Our Lady Queen Of Peace Catholic Engineering College, Skelmersdale

JMO

The JMO has lots of football pitches,
It is just down the road from Sandy Lane,
You can play football there, it is good to go with mates.

When Skelmersdale are playing at the JMO,
Everybody goes to watch them,
And the atmosphere is really good because everybody joins in.

The goals are made out of metal and the netting is really strong too,
There is also a bar to go to at the JMO after you've finished playing football.
They have fake grass, so the grass is always really good and nice.

Jack Douglas (12)
Our Lady Queen Of Peace Catholic Engineering College, Skelmersdale

In Blackpool

In Blackpool, there are beaches and amusement parks,
In Blackpool, people have many things to do,
Blackpool is in Lancashire, near the Irish Sea.

Blackpool is crowded and amazing,
Pleasure Beach is exciting and loud,
The arcades are fun and dark.

I can see the golden beach, blue sea and white seagulls,
I can hear cars going by and people talking to each other,
Here, I feel happy.

And I,
Would love to visit again,
In Blackpool, there are beaches and amusement parks.

Shayla-Mae Lewin (12)
Our Lady Queen Of Peace Catholic Engineering College, Skelmersdale

The Climate Crisis

The air began to pollute
Humans began to destroy
The greenhouse gases are released
We are going to increase
The temperature of the Earth

We increase the Earth's population
We build more houses
We build mega cities
We are polluting the Earth
The sea levels rise
These cities won't survive

We sweat and sweat
The heat is too much
Stop and think where
Your rubbish goes when you litter
This is it, no Planet B
Make sure you save the trees.

Kyran Crosbie (12)
Our Lady Queen Of Peace Catholic Engineering College, Skelmersdale

Disastrous Deforestation

The trees are being cut down
We must go against this
This is harming our world
Some animals that are getting affected by this are birds, monkeys, orangutans and reptiles such as snakes
The people who cut down trees do not realise what they are doing
We must put an end to this

The more we cut down trees the more carbon dioxide is being released
Which can lead to the greenhouse effect
Which starts to make all the polar ice caps melt down and
Leads to towns/cities/countries flooding.

Charlie Poulton (12)
Our Lady Queen Of Peace Catholic Engineering College, Skelmersdale

Everton: No Spirit Left For The Blues

Sometimes I feel like not liking them anymore,
The depression and sadness it brings, just place us in League 2.
Next season, we'll be playing Boreham Wood weekly,
The tactics don't work any longer, no longer ticking like clockwork.
The fans give up, our time's nearly up,
Come on Frank, pick us back up.
The team just don't believe what could be,
The future is now, a long-forgotten dream.
Everton, there's no hope for the blues,
Everton, we're just going to lose!

Leon Forkin (13)
Our Lady Queen Of Peace Catholic Engineering College, Skelmersdale

Blackpool Fair

Blackpool fair has a pub,
As people go on rides and adults get drunk,
This fair is on a pier.

This fair is loud but joyful,
The pier is long and sturdy,
The rides are alive and magical.

You can see every colour of the rainbow,
You can hear the laughter and screaming from people having fun,
You can hear the calm ocean swaying along the beach,
I feel awake, excited and joyful.

And I...
Feel that the pier is for every age,
Blackpool fair has a pub.

Emily Boden (12)
Our Lady Queen Of Peace Catholic Engineering College, Skelmersdale

Blackpool Fair

Blackpool has a fair,
There are people in the air,
It is near the beach.

The beach is huge and exciting,
The beach is relaxing and sunny,
The rides have a wonderful, surprising view.

The colours everywhere are red, pink, green and blue,
The sounds of the birds chirping and the rides clanging,
I feel butterflies in my stomach and I feel a bit anxious.

And I...
Imagine kids screaming, laughing and shouting with joy and happiness,
Blackpool has a fair.

Emily Johnson (12)
Our Lady Queen Of Peace Catholic Engineering College, Skelmersdale

Save Our World

Our world is dying,
Animals are crying.
We are causing pain,
Ruining the food chain.
Soon we will have no world!
What can we do?

Take a seat,
Think about the heat.
The ice caps are melting,
No animals are settling.
Many creatures are going extinct too!
What can we do?

Our litter going into the sea,
Causing an underwater disease.
Sharks being used for only their fins,
People committing terrible sins.
Lord, save our world.

Tayla Caveney (12)
Our Lady Queen Of Peace Catholic Engineering College, Skelmersdale

Help Ukraine

U kraine needs help
K ids are having to leave their country
R ussia needs to be stopped
A ll the people living in Ukraine need help
I nnocent people are being killed
N o one deserves to go through this
E veryone should be able to live peacefully

W hen people are being killed it's ruining their family
A ll the families in Ukraine are not living peacefully
R oaring sound of gunfire.

Kian Cooper (13)
Our Lady Queen Of Peace Catholic Engineering College, Skelmersdale

The War In Ukraine

The sunflowers blossom out,
While Putin's on the pout.
Even though it's a wholesome place,
While it's a race to defeat one another.
While people are in danger and despair,
We're out here enjoying the fresh air.
When they die,
They will fly.
Up to Heaven, they'll go,
Where no war will follow.
RIP to those who have died.
Putin is a monster,
Manipulating a nation,
God bless Ukraine and those in it.

Lucas Standrell (13)
Our Lady Queen Of Peace Catholic Engineering College, Skelmersdale

Anfield: You'll Never Walk Alone

Anfield is a wonderful place,
Watching Liverpool play with my own eyes,
Liverpool's stadium is right next to Goodison Park.

Anfield is beautiful and enormous,
The views from inside are exhilarating,
The pitch is very green and clean.

Red, green, white and blue,
I can hear the crowd chanting,
The feeling is like I'm dreaming.

And I,
Feel like Anfield is my home,
Anfield is a wonderful place.

Noah Connaughton (12)
Our Lady Queen Of Peace Catholic Engineering College, Skelmersdale

Christmas

C hildren waiting for Santa
H opefully the dog doesn't eat Santa's food
R udolph guiding the way with his shiny nose
I can see the gingerbread men looking so nice
S tockings are full and hung on the fireplace
T rees all lit up and decorated with presents underneath
M ums getting the reindeer dust
A ll the family gathering around
S anta fell down the chimney and got stuck.

Chloe Fitzpatrick (14)
Our Lady Queen Of Peace Catholic Engineering College, Skelmersdale

The Real Me

No one knows the real me,
Whenever I'm alone I feel like a dark cloud.
Whenever I'm with people I act like someone different.
Everyone thinks I'm one way, but I'm not.
Everyone thinks they know me, but no one really does.
A false face hides what a false heart knows,
Moods change when the wind blows.
No one knows the real me but this is who I really am,
No one knows who I am.
This is the way I actually feel.

Sophie McHale (13)
Our Lady Queen Of Peace Catholic Engineering College, Skelmersdale

Christmas Time

C hildren excited for Santa to come
H opeful that Santa won't get lost
R udolph guiding the way with his bright red nose
I can smell gingerbread
S tockings hung up on the fireplace
T he tree is all lit up with presents all around
M um is making Christmas dinner
A ll the family gathered around the table
S ome would say it's the most wonderful time of the year!

Courtney Felton (13)
Our Lady Queen Of Peace Catholic Engineering College, Skelmersdale

What's Going On?

U sing violence, I don't know what is going on
K illing innocent people - Putin, what have you done?
R aiding countries like it's 1942
A ll the soldiers dying, mothers in grief, crying
I n my eyes, this is all wrong; war is never the way to go
N ATO is trying to help Ukraine because Putin is not stopping
E veryone screaming, fearing for their lives, afraid they're going to die.

Ryan Wright (13)
Our Lady Queen Of Peace Catholic Engineering College, Skelmersdale

Wigan Stadium

Wigan Stadium has a footy pitch,
Wigan Stadium hosts games,
Wigan Stadium is located in Wigan.

The stadium is quiet but loud,
The pitch is sleek and bright,
The seats however are rusty and old.

You can see green, red, white and blue,
You can hear the wind pass by you,
You feel pride looking at the pitch.

And I,
Think that this is a beautiful place,
Wigan has a footy pitch.

Mieszko Beczkiewicz (12)
Our Lady Queen Of Peace Catholic Engineering College, Skelmersdale

Eco Issues

E ndangered animals are endangered and need help
C limate change getting worse
O ur planet needs saving and fast

I ce caps melting quicker so Antarctica will soon be gone
S eas getting larger because of the ice melting
S torms getting more dangerous and life threatening
U nderwater animals are dying
E arth is slowly fading away
S ea levels rising.

Lexi Sultan (12)
Our Lady Queen Of Peace Catholic Engineering College, Skelmersdale

Climate Change

I believe we can stop climate change,
If we recycle and reuse things we buy.
We can also help by stopping deforestation,
We can also try to help China with its air pollution,
And the overworking they're having to do.
It's our responsibility to keep our world safe, not destroy it.
People may think, *we won't protect it because nothing will happen*,
But we are destroying our Earth, one by one.

Ruby Kervin (12)
Our Lady Queen Of Peace Catholic Engineering College, Skelmersdale

Christmas

C hristmas decorations on every house
H earty Christmas dinner is being prepared
R udolph has eaten the carrots we left out
I can see a gingerbread house on the table
S anta coming down the chimney
T ree decorating is very fun
M um has been wrapping the presents
A ll the family gathering around the tree
S tockings have been filled in the night.

Sadie Gleave (13)
Our Lady Queen Of Peace Catholic Engineering College, Skelmersdale

The Death Of The Queen

The Queen died,
The world cried.
It's like we've lost our nan,
She reigned for 70 years,
Everyone was a fan.
Before she died, she enjoyed a marmalade sandwich,
Paddington was there,
They shared a few words.
The children watched on,
As they said, "Mum, the Queen met Paddington."
A few months later, she passed.
Rest in peace, Elizabeth.
You went too fast.

Aimee Worrall (14)
Our Lady Queen Of Peace Catholic Engineering College, Skelmersdale

Fake

H appiness doesn't come from love
A ll love isn't real, be careful who you trust
P lease let me out of this trap
P lease, it's nearly been a year
I can't suffer from this pain anymore
N ot even one more day
E verything he said was fake
S top using me as a game when you are
S ick and tired of your other girls.

Jessie Parker (13)
Our Lady Queen Of Peace Catholic Engineering College, Skelmersdale

Living Nowadays

Cost of living is really high
Some people go hungry because of costs
Feels like everyday prices are getting higher
What are we going to do?
I believe in the next ten years our population will decrease by millions
We're not going to be able to afford it
What can we do?
We need to fight for our future
Help our world!
Help our people!
How can we sort these prices?

Amy-Dee Brow (13)
Our Lady Queen Of Peace Catholic Engineering College, Skelmersdale

Liverpool Central

Liverpool Central has shops,
People going from shop to shop,
Inside the centre of Liverpool.

The centre is huge and cool,
Kenji is quiet and bright,
The glass floor is tall and scary.

Brown, green and yellow,
Shoppers shuffle, sit and eat,
I feel happy here.

And I,
I feel like I belong in this wonderful place,
Liverpool Central has shops.

Thomas Massam (12)
Our Lady Queen Of Peace Catholic Engineering College, Skelmersdale

Halloween

H alloween parties with family and friends
W **A** iting for the excited trick-or-treaters
L istening to spooky songs
P **L** aying Halloween games
Trick **O** r treating around the block
W itches with hats bigger than their heads
E vil spirits floating around
D **E** corating your house all scary
N ew horror films to watch with family.

Ava Tilley (13)
Our Lady Queen Of Peace Catholic Engineering College, Skelmersdale

Bullying = Danger = Terrifying

B orn not looking how you want
U nder a dark cloud, the victim sits
L ies spread around your head like speech bubbles
L ooking and waiting where hell waits for you
Y elling inwardly for help
I n your dreams, you are free of the pain
N ot leaving your home out of fear and anxiety
'G etting over it' is not an option.

Liam Gadsby (13)
Our Lady Queen Of Peace Catholic Engineering College, Skelmersdale

Survive The Night

P eople living on the streets while others in castles
O ften feeling cold and hungry
V ery expensive food you barely afford
E veryone caring about themselves, never you
R ight to food and warmth, they say
T ogether we can fight this and help you
Y ou might know how it feels, let's make sure no one else does. Let's fight this.

Roksana Spira (13)
Our Lady Queen Of Peace Catholic Engineering College, Skelmersdale

Climate Change

Whilst greenhouse gases are going up into the atmosphere,
The climate is getting dearer and dearer.
As the ice melts down the drain,
The sea level rises up again.
The trees decreasing rapidly,
Carbon dioxide rising up quickly.
If we don't stop this now,
It will go on forever.
Dump this climate change in the bin,
And get a better life to play with.

Archie Elliott-Tynon
Our Lady Queen Of Peace Catholic Engineering College, Skelmersdale

Energy Bills Are Skyrocketing

E veryone needs a warm home
N obody should have to sleep in a freezing bed
E nergy bills are skyrocketing
R aging parents
G iving defrosted food
Y our aunties and uncles stressing

B eing bored
I n total darkness
L ittle heat
L ong nights
S tarving families have little food.

Libby Baines (13)
Our Lady Queen Of Peace Catholic Engineering College, Skelmersdale

War In Ukraine

W e are worried
A re we in danger?
R easons for leaving are plenty

I s it ending soon?
N obody feels safe

U kraine needs help
K eep on supporting
R each out to Ukrainians
A lot of lives lost
I s it going to end?
N obody can go
E very day is a challenge.

Lee O'Brien (13)
Our Lady Queen Of Peace Catholic Engineering College, Skelmersdale

Action

P eople all around are living in poverty
O ften feeling hungry at night
V ery young people's families can't afford healthcare
E ven though we have a warm home to go
R ight now there are people starving
T o our future generations, you will not live like this anymore
Y our lives are now our responsibility.

Darcey Kelly (13)
Our Lady Queen Of Peace Catholic Engineering College, Skelmersdale

The Crisis On The Streets

P eople are dying all over the world,
V ery tired and often hurled,
O ften hungry and scared for their life,
E veryone walking past through the night,
R unning away from the dark to light,
T hen the people can't believe their sight,
Y ou and others just don't dare, to question their filthy care.

Brooke Fenney (13)
Our Lady Queen Of Peace Catholic Engineering College, Skelmersdale

The Environment

E nvironment matters
N ature
V icious hunts
I f we don't help now, who will?
R ace against time
O veruse of plastic
N obody should leave litter on the floor
M ake a difference
E veryone needs to help
N ever hurt the animals
T he future isn't bright.

Lily Bennett (13)
Our Lady Queen Of Peace Catholic Engineering College, Skelmersdale

Climate Change

Climate change is all around us,
If you can't see it, open your eyes.
The people in charge of our world,
Are hiding behind their smiles and lies.
When we are asleep,
The trees become weak.
As the heat doesn't belong,
With old trees, it's just wrong.
Our Earth is burning,
But everyone has stopped caring.

Eva Nolan (12)
Our Lady Queen Of Peace Catholic Engineering College, Skelmersdale

Recycling

R euse things that are in stable condition
E nable a better life
C reate new items, things, toys
Y ou can give people in need what you don't use
C onvince people to recycle too; reduce, reuse, recycle
L eave your rubbish in the correct bins
E stablish a good lifestyle and go green.

Aira Tetero (12)
Our Lady Queen Of Peace Catholic Engineering College, Skelmersdale

I Miss My Dad

I miss my dad
It's been two months since he went
Where did he go?
Mum says business and work
My friends say they know
Where he truly went
But I think it's lies
He doesn't like violence and threats
He wouldn't dare shoot a gun
Or mess around with big old bombs
They're wrong for a fact.

Mikołaj Spyra (13)
Our Lady Queen Of Peace Catholic Engineering College, Skelmersdale

The Environmental Problem

E ndangered animals
N uclear waste
V iolent fires
I nspire others to recycle trash and waste
R aining bombs
O n our shoulders a huge responsibility
N ever-ending problems
M elting ice
E normous waves
N o one is safe
T he world is dying.

Kerija Klauberga (13)
Our Lady Queen Of Peace Catholic Engineering College, Skelmersdale

Prices Are Poo

P rices are high
R ations to eat
I ll all the time
C upboards empty
E venings so cold
S tarting to weep

A t night I freeze
R aging breeze
E ver will it end

P lease go down
O ur money is gone
O ne of you listen.

Ethan Dwyer (13)
Our Lady Queen Of Peace Catholic Engineering College, Skelmersdale

Torn Till End

Being torn to bits and pieces,
Feeling alone only with my thoughts.
Getting laughed at for who I am,
Wanting to be gone.
I must be strong.
Acting happy with people I love,
The dark cloud forms above.
Yet everyone else shining above,
Nobody knows how I feel.
Just wait until my thoughts become real.

Sarah Massam (13)
Our Lady Queen Of Peace Catholic Engineering College, Skelmersdale

Eco Poem

C arbon footprint
L ayers in rainforest
I ntense storms
M elting ice caps
A nimals going extinct
T yphoons
E missions

C old
H ope
A rid areas
N utrients
G reenhouse effect
E lectric cars.

Dan Saver (13)
Our Lady Queen Of Peace Catholic Engineering College, Skelmersdale

Stop Bullying

B e confident and speak out
U se your mind and don't be in doubt
L ove your friends
L ove them till the end
Y ou are so special
I need you so much
N ever leave or it will be rough
G o, don't go and for me it will be rough.

Leo Bacon (14)
Our Lady Queen Of Peace Catholic Engineering College, Skelmersdale

Stop Bullying

B e kind to everybody
U nderstand people's problems
L earn how to help others
L ook out for your friends
Y our friends should look out for you
I nclude everyone
N ever let someone tell you what to do
G row to make new friends.

Lily Heyes (13)
Our Lady Queen Of Peace Catholic Engineering College, Skelmersdale

An Endangered Creature

Roses are red, violets are blue,
Our lovely animals are getting killed because of you.
How many times do we have to say stop,
Before our world is ruined?
For the benefit of everyone,
Stop poaching, stop deforestation, stop polluting
And treat the world like you want to be treated.

Oscar Finegan (12)
Our Lady Queen Of Peace Catholic Engineering College, Skelmersdale

Poverty Is A Big Problem In Society

P eople dying from starvation
O ften hungry at night time
V ile politicians taxing the poor
E mpty stomach without food or drink
R eally thirsty and sick with no money to treat the illness
T errible lifestyle
Y et starvation strikes again.

Connor White (13)
Our Lady Queen Of Peace Catholic Engineering College, Skelmersdale

Recycling

I believe we can recycle,
Yes, that includes you, Michael.
It's time to pick up and clean,
To keep our planet green.
It's easy when you know what bin,
From cardboard to plastic and tin.
We all need to act and do our part,
You all know what to do deep in your heart.

Lily Lowe (13)
Our Lady Queen Of Peace Catholic Engineering College, Skelmersdale

Trolling

Cyberbullying
No escape from the trolling
It makes people feel sad
So don't be bad
Don't be a bully
Because it's not funny
Cyberbullying can cause
Really serious mental health problems
Don't be the cause
Of someone's death.

Summer Chadwick (13)
Our Lady Queen Of Peace Catholic Engineering College, Skelmersdale

Empty Pockets

P eople are suffering more and more
O pen up if you need help
V ery hard times
E veryone feels the same
R esilience isn't always the way
T oday is gonna be a great day
Y ou don't always have to worry.

Jack Bradbury (13)
Our Lady Queen Of Peace Catholic Engineering College, Skelmersdale

Save The Future

F or the next generation
U nderstanding the environment
T errible heat melting ice caps
U se electric instead of gas
R emember, don't rely on the future, rely on yourself
E veryone needs a good life.

Alfie Wilson (13)
Our Lady Queen Of Peace Catholic Engineering College, Skelmersdale

Climate Change: Recycling!

R euse plastic
E cosystem
C limate change
Y ears of recycling
C hanges in the world
L ooking after our planet
I nternational
N o recycling damages the Earth
G reen.

Sienna Grice (12)
Our Lady Queen Of Peace Catholic Engineering College, Skelmersdale

Climate Change: Recycling

R euse plastic
E cosystem
C limate change
Y ears of recycling
C hanges in the world
L ooking after our world
I think
N o recycling
G reatly damages the Earth.

Ruby Lewis (13)
Our Lady Queen Of Peace Catholic Engineering College, Skelmersdale

My Music

My music
Music is my safe space
It helps me escape
All my troubles are gone when I press play
Oh, how I wish to be in a different place
But that doesn't matter as long as I have my music.

Leah Smith (13)
Our Lady Queen Of Peace Catholic Engineering College, Skelmersdale

Thai Boxing

M uay Thai is a martial art
U nder the ceiling, it is taught
A nd it is used in UFC
Y our martial art is like a new start - use it and you will see.

Aiden Fallon (13)
Our Lady Queen Of Peace Catholic Engineering College, Skelmersdale

Stop Littering

I believe we can stop climate change,
If we can recycle and reuse,
All of the stuff we buy in the shops.

Lucy Gilbertson (12)
Our Lady Queen Of Peace Catholic Engineering College, Skelmersdale

Young Writers
Est. 1991

Young Writers Information

We hope you have enjoyed reading this book – and that you will continue to in the coming years.

If you're the parent or family member of an enthusiastic poet or story writer, do visit our website **www.youngwriters.co.uk/subscribe** and sign up to receive news, competitions, writing challenges and tips, activities and much, much more! There's lots to keep budding writers motivated!

If you would like to order further copies of this book, or any of our other titles, then please give us a call or order via your online account.

Young Writers
Remus House
Coltsfoot Drive
Peterborough
PE2 9BF
(01733) 890066
info@youngwriters.co.uk

Join in the conversation!
Tips, news, giveaways and much more!

YoungWritersUK   **YoungWritersCW**   **youngwriterscw**